Angry Ninja
ACTIVITY BOOK

Ninja Life Hacks™

Welcome

Hello there, ninjas! I'm Angry Ninja and this is my activity book. It's packed with everything from puzzles to coloring and fill-in fun!

This book belongs to:

....

....

There are lots of ways to express yourself! Let's check it out.

FEELING FRUSTRATED?

That's okay. It's totally normal to feel angry sometimes. Inside this book, you will discover new ways to deal with your anger and celebrate your different emotions. As well as puzzles, there are helpful mindfulness and breathing techniques for you to try out, too! And the best thing about them is that you can use these tools wherever you go—they can be your secret weapon to feeling in control of your emotions.

Contents

All about me!

Grab your pens and pencils to fill in these pages with everything about YOU!

My name is ....

I am .... years old.

I live in ....

I live with ....

....

....

Check the words that describe you:

- ☐ Confident
- ☐ Stressed
- ☐ Noisy
- ☐ Kind
- ☐ Friendly
- ☐ Grumpy
- ☐ Quiet

My eye color ....

My hair color ....

My hair is

short ☐   medium ☐   long ☐

I am

short ☐   medium height ☐   tall ☐

My favorite colors are . . .

Color them in!

Do you get angry sometimes?
Draw your angry self here . . .

This is what I look like
when I get mad!

Ninja Life Hacks™

All about me!

My best friends are . . .

....

....

....

....

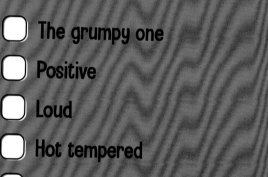

My friends would say that I'm. . .

- ☐ The grumpy one
- ☐ Positive
- ☐ Loud
- ☐ Hot tempered
- ☐ Funny
- ☐ Kind
- ☐ Angry
- ☐ Athletic
- ☐ Creative
- ☐ Bold

What do you prefer?

(YOU CAN ONLY CIRCLE ONE EACH TIME!)

SWEET   or   SALTY

LOTS OF NOISE
or
PEACE AND QUIET

OUT AND ABOUT
or
STAYING INSIDE

SPORTS   or   MUSIC

BOOKS   or   TV

DRAWING   or   DANCING

PARK   or   MUSEUM

COOKIES   or   CAKE

SPRING   or   FALL

Complete each sentence by circling your top choices.

1. I would choose a pet . . .

HAMSTER / HORSE / GOLDFISH / LIZARD

2. I would choose to live . . .

BY A LAKE / IN THE MOUNTAINS / IN A CITY

3. I would choose . . .

BOOKS / TV / MOVIES / DRAWING

4. I would choose to go . . .

WALKING / SWIMMING / BIKING / RUNNING

5. I would choose to play . . .

OUTDOORS / INDOORS

WHY DON'T YOU TRY THESE QUESTIONS ON YOUR FRIENDS AND FAMILY, TOO?

All about me!

Check the things you like to do in your spare time!

- ☐ Painting or drawing
- ☐ Hanging out with friends
- ☐ Playing sports
- ☐ Watching TV
- ☐ Baking or cooking

My Favorites

Snack: ....

TV show: ....

Movie: ....

Season: ....

Animal: ....

Person: ....

Book: ....

THINGS THAT MAKE ME ANGRY!

(Check the ones that make you feel mad, then write some of your own.)

- [ ] Feeling hungry
- [ ] People who are unkind
- [ ] Making mistakes
- [ ] When I can't do things
- [ ] ....
- [ ] ....
- [ ] ....
- [ ] ....
- [ ] ....

HAPPY THINGS!

(Check the ones that make you feel good, then write some of your own.)

- [ ] Listening to music
- [ ] Going for a walk
- [ ] Time with friends
- [ ] Telling jokes
- [ ] Helping people
- [ ] ....
- [ ] ....
- [ ] ....
- [ ] ....
- [ ] ....

COLOR JOURNAL

Use this page to record all of the things you've done lately. Color in as many clouds as you like, and then talk about each one with your grownup!

Shouted at my best friend

Felt frightened

Went to bed early

Had a good day at school

Told the truth

Felt shy

Cried

Had fun with my family

Felt happy

Had fun with a friend

Had an argument with my family

Felt nervous

Had a great idea

Laughed

Felt excited

Made something

Felt like giving up

Helped out at home

Broke something

Made a mistake

Had a bad day at school

Felt sad

Read a book

Went to bed late

Watched TV

Told a lie

CLUES FROM WITHIN

Anger is a big emotion. You can look out for signs that you're getting angry by noticing these signals that your body sends out!

CAN YOU MATCH EACH DESCRIPTION TO THE RIGHT BODY PART? DRAW LINES TO LABEL THE PICTURE.

EYEBROWS LOW AND DRAWN TOGETHER

EYE MUSCLES TIGHTEN

HEART BEATS FASTER

FEEL LIKE SCREAMING

HUNCHED SHOULDERS

CLENCHED FISTS

I FEEL ANGRY WHEN . . .

There are lots of reasons why you might feel angry. Look at Angry Ninja's ideas and color in any of them that sound like you.

SAY A POSITIVE MESSAGE TO YOURSELF WHENEVER YOU FEEL DISCOURAGED!

something is too difficult

I am tired

I am hungry

I get told off

I feel silly

people laugh at me

somebody takes my stuff without asking

I don't understand something

somebody is mean to me

I'm. So. Angry!

I make mistakes

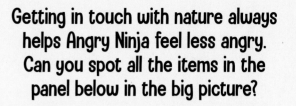

SEARCH AND FIND

Getting in touch with nature always helps Angry Ninja feel less angry. Can you spot all the items in the panel below in the big picture?

ADD A NINJA STICKER NEXT TO EACH ITEM WHEN YOU SPOT THEM IN THE BIG PICTURE.

GET OUTSIDE

Playing sports or running around outdoors can be a good way to release anger in a positive way.

COLOR IN THE NINJAS USING YOUR BRIGHTEST COLORED PENCILS OR CRAYONS.

HERE'S AN EXAMPLE OF COLORS YOU COULD USE!

WORD SEARCH

How quickly can you find and circle all of the angry words in the grid below? Check each word off as you go!

F	J	L	C	X	J	Q	Z	X	A	Z	G	D	A	M
R	D	P	P	M	S	C	L	N	V	I	E	N	Z	J
U	P	E	S	F	P	U	G	C	D	E	Z	K	P	M
S	R	V	Y	W	U	R	D	E	S	S	E	R	T	S
T	T	A	L	O	Y	R	T	L	W	O	V	G	I	Y
R	E	T	G	F	N	A	I	J	J	T	N	Y	O	H
A	T	K	U	I	T	N	O	O	R	O	X	Q	Y	H
T	C	Q	J	I	N	N	A	I	U	C	R	O	S	S
E	H	M	R	C	X	G	L	D	L	S	O	N	W	W
D	Y	R	D	Y	Z	E	V	I	S	O	L	P	X	E
T	I	Q	J	U	D	O	P	G	U	U	C	M	Q	U
F	U	M	I	N	G	E	N	C	P	X	P	P	D	P
I	Y	X	X	J	R	Q	E	H	N	N	D	A	I	S
U	M	Q	E	C	O	J	S	F	F	F	Y	U	I	E
D	S	E	H	V	H	J	I	A	C	V	Y	Z	O	T

- ◯ CROSS
- ◯ FURIOUS
- ◯ FRUSTRATED
- ◯ ANGRY
- ◯ STRESSED
- ◯ ANNOYED
- ◯ MAD
- ◯ IRRITATED
- ◯ FUMING
- ◯ RAGING
- ◯ UPSET
- ◯ EXPLOSIVE

How did this activity make YOU feel?

Add a thumbs up or a thumbs down sticker here. ↘

CRACK THE CODES

Use the colorful code wheel to reveal the secret ninja messages on the opposite page. They will help you to deal with your feelings when you get angry!

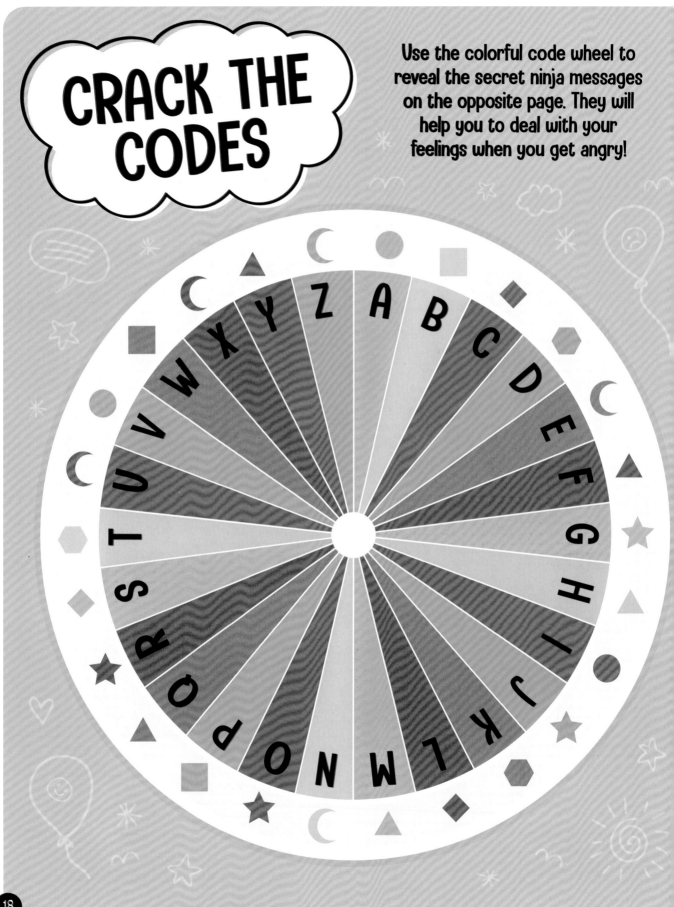

HAPPY TIMES

Take a moment to think about a joyful time. Maybe you had an amazing day out at the beach, or you played games with your friends—it can be whatever you like! Doodle a picture of your happy memory in the space below and color it in.

IF YOU DON'T WANT TO DRAW, YOU COULD WRITE ABOUT IT INSTEAD.

Good memories always make me feel happier!

COLOR IT OUT

Now think about something that made you feel angry. Doodle a picture of it and then color it in.

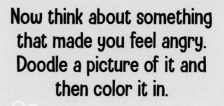

If I'm in a bad mood, sometimes it helps to let it out!

How did this activity make YOU feel?

Add a thumbs up or a thumbs down sticker here. ⟶

MAKE IT MATCH

Look carefully at both pictures. There are 8 differences to spot. After you spot the differences, draw in the things that are missing from picture B to make the two scenes match.

B

Add a lightning bolt sticker below for every difference you spot.

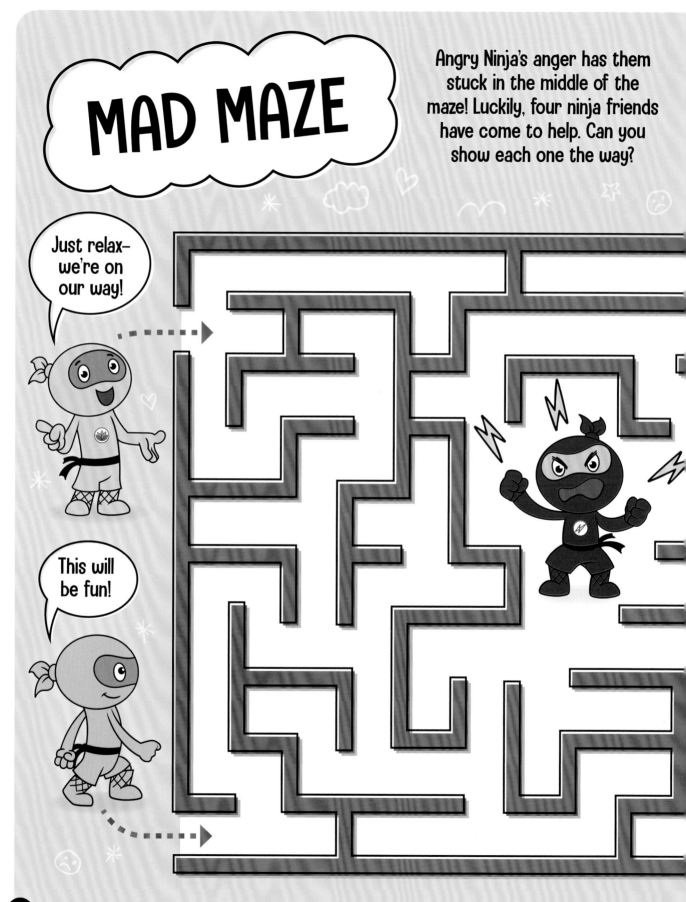

SHADOW MATCHING

Strike a pose!
Draw lines to match up the pictures of Angry Ninja to the correct shadows. Don't forget to color in the ninjas!

TIME OUT

Sometimes anger can bubble up and make you feel like you have no control. Try out this simple technique to get your power back!

All you need is one minute for this technique.

WHAT TO DO:
Stop and focus on what's around you. Then answer these simple questions:

What can I see? ....

What can I hear? ....

What can I smell? ....

What can I feel? ....

What can I taste? ....

ANGRY ME!

The next time you feel angry, notice what it does to your body. Circle the words that describe how your anger feels. You could add your own words, too.

EYES:
Wide / Scrunched up

....

FACE:
Hot / Sweaty

....
....

EARS:
Hot / Itchy

....

MOUTH:
Tight jaw /
Gritted teeth

....
....

HANDS:
Clenched fists /
Hot / Cold

....
....

FEET:
Curled toes / Hot / Cold

....

BELLY:
Sick / Churning feeling

....

DOT-TO-DOT

Connect the dots to finish this picture of Angry Ninja, then add the lightning bolt emblem, and color in your creation!

CAN YOU SPOT IT?

Time spent doing fun things with friends helps Angry Ninja to feel less stressed and angry! There are 7 differences between these two pictures to spot. How many can you find?

Add a star sticker below for every difference you spot.

COLOR 'N' BREATHE

Breathing exercises can help to calm angry feelings. Fill in each band of the rainbow using a different color, then try the breathing exercise below.

BREATHING EXERCISE:

1. Follow the red arrow to trace your finger over the first band of color, and take a slow, deep breath in. Pause.

2. Now follow the green arrow back along the next band of color while slowly breathing out.

3. Repeat this for each band. You can do the exercise as many times as you like!

BREATHE IN

BREATHE OUT

How did this activity make YOU feel?

Add a thumbs up or a thumbs down sticker here.

START

COMPLETE THE JIGSAW

Draw in the missing puzzle pieces to complete this picture of Angry Ninja, then color it in.

WHAT WOULD CALM NINJA DO?

Unlike Angry Ninja, Calm Ninja always tries to keep cool, no matter what! Circle the emotion that Calm Ninja is showing in each situation.

Trying to eat a popsicle while getting bothered by bees!

WORRIED

or

CHILL

It's ok. If I stay still, they'll leave me alone.

Accidentally making a mess!

CALM

or

UPSET

Discovering that someone has eaten all the sweets!

ANGRY or **COOL**

Would you like another one?

Ooops!

Learning to play the drums!

EXCITED or **MAD**

How did this activity make you feel? Add a thumbs up or a thumbs down sticker here.

FACE IT

Draw the different emotions on the blank faces to complete these ninjas!

ANGRY

CALM

NERVOUS

ZEN

WHICH NINJA ARE YOU TODAY? ADD A HAPPY FACE STICKER NEXT TO ONE OF THEM.

GUIDED COLORING

Think about how these things would make you feel? Color the stars in red if they make you feel angry, or color them green if they make you feel calm.

ANGRY

CALM

I helped my friend

I lost in a game

I made a new friend

Someone used my stuff without asking

I listened to my favorite song

I asked somebody to play with me

Somebody broke my things

My friend helped me

My friends wouldn't let me join in

I watched my favorite movie

My friend laughed at me

I went to bed early

I got in trouble

I got lost

I ate my favorite food

Write your own words in the blank stars. Then color them in either red or green!

FEISTY PHRASES

Can you think of angry words or phrases that start with these letters? Write them in the blank spaces to complete this puzzle.

A
N
G
R
Y

HERE ARE SOME IDEAS FOR INSPIRATION!

A nnoyed
R age

How did this activity make YOU feel?

Add a thumbs up or a thumbs down sticker here.

STAR GAZING

Gazing at the stars can be a relaxing way to end the day. Fill the scene with stickers of planets, moons, and shooting stars. Then draw your own objects in the sky to complete the scene.

SPECIAL SURPRISE

Kind Ninja and Caring Ninja want to cheer up Angry Ninja with a special surprise! What do you think it could be? Draw it in the space below.

PERHAPS IT'S A CUPCAKE OR A FLOWER!

Wow, I think Angry Ninja will love this!

HIDDEN MESSAGE

Angry Ninja is trying to figure out what this message from Calm Ninja says. Cross out the correct letters in each row to reveal each word!

This message will help Angry Ninja!

Cross out all of the letters that are not in PINK circles.

V A C L R W U A D Y B S T

....

Cross out all of the letters in PURPLE circles.

Y R S E T M F E O M D B X E W R U

....

Cross out all of the letters that are not in YELLOW circles.

R B T R S O C A

....

Thank you, Calm Ninja!

Cross out all of the letters in ORANGE circles.

R B F R S E C A A T Y H K E S

....

43

COOL DOWN

Calm Ninja is showing Angry Ninja a breathing exercise to use whenever things feel like they're getting too stressful. Color in each ninja and try the breathing technique for yourself!

THE MOST IMPORTANT THING ABOUT STAYING CALM IS REMEMBERING TO BREATHE.

A calm mind is the ultimate weapon to handle life's challenges.

MINDFUL MANTRA

Are you having a bad day? Sometimes reading positive phrases can change your mood for the better and lift your spirits. Come up with some words and phrases to read and say out loud.

MY MANTRAS!

....

....

....

....

....

....

....

....

....

....

YOU COULD USE SOME OF THESE SUGGESTIONS, OR JUST MAKE UP YOUR OWN.

IDEAS

I will!

I am calm!

I can do this!

I try my best!

WRITE SOME OF YOUR FAVORITE MANTRAS ON A PIECE OF PAPER AND KEEP THEM NEXT TO YOUR BED OR IN YOUR BACKPACK. THEY CAN BE YOUR SECRET WEAPON WHEN YOU FEEL DISCOURAGED.

ODD ONE OUT

Angry Ninja is feeling mad after dropping an ice cream. Help Angry Ninja by choosing a new treat. Check the odd one out in each row.

1. A B C

2. A B C

3. A B C

INNER CALM

Use the ideas on this list to help you find your inner calm—it's packed with things to try when you feel angry or frustrated.

CHECK THESE OFF WHEN YOU TRY EACH ONE. USE THEM AS INSPIRATION FOR GOALS TO TRY!

- [ ] Drink a glass of water
- [ ] Paint a picture
- [ ] Do some stretches
- [ ] Count to 10
- [ ] Do some coloring
- [ ] Listen to my favorite music
- [ ] Breathe in and out deeply, three times
- [ ] Draw something
- [ ] Read a book

- [ ] Tell my grownup how I feel

- [ ] Think of something silly that makes me giggle

- [ ] Look for shapes in the clouds

- [ ] Write in a journal

- [ ] Go for a walk

- [ ] Do a silly dance

Write your own ideas here:

DRAW IT

Doing something creative like drawing can help you feel less frustrated and angry. Draw Angry Ninja using the grid to help you. Don't forget to color in your picture!

DRAWING CAN HELP YOU TO FOCUS IF YOU FEEL DISTRACTED. IT CAN ALSO HELP YOU TO EXPRESS HOW YOU'RE FEELING!

BLOW AWAY YOUR ANGER

What are some things that make you feel angry? Write them down in the bubbles on this page. Then close your eyes and imagine blowing them all away, and watching them disappear into the universe.

YOU CAN DO THIS WHENEVER YOU WANT AND WHEREVER YOU ARE. YOU DON'T EVEN NEED A PIECE OF PAPER—JUST IMAGINE EACH WORRY IN A BUBBLE!

When I write angry thoughts down, sometimes I realize they're not so bad after all.

How did this activity make YOU feel?

Add a thumbs up or a thumbs down sticker here.

TO CALM CORNER!

Follow the trail and complete all of the activities to help Angry Ninja reach Calm Corner. Help out the ninja friends along the way!

START

This had better not take too long.

Draw lines to match up the pairs.

Color in the game controller so the left side is the mirror image of the right.

How many ninjas can you count hiding on these pages? Write your answer in the space.

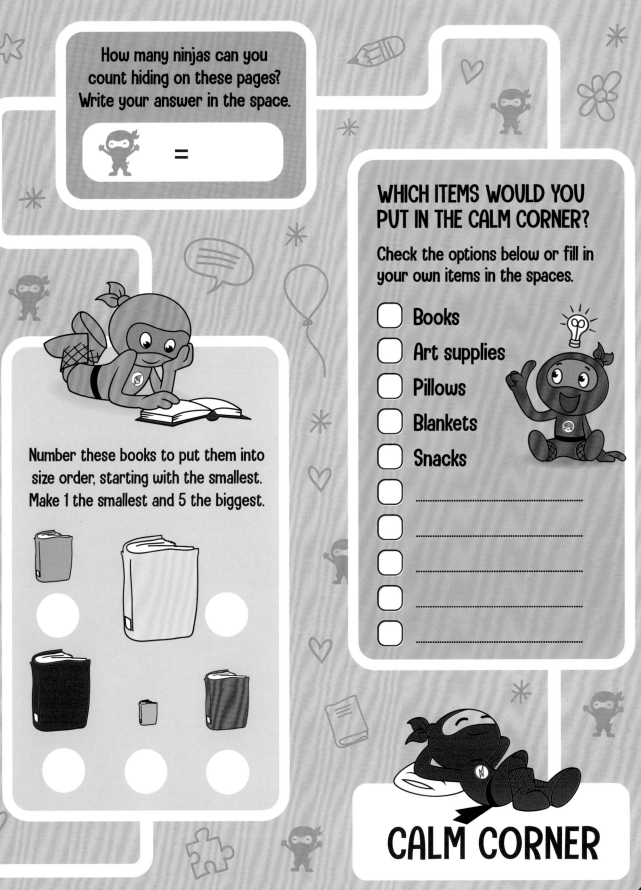

=

WHICH ITEMS WOULD YOU PUT IN THE CALM CORNER?

Check the options below or fill in your own items in the spaces.

- ☐ Books
- ☐ Art supplies
- ☐ Pillows
- ☐ Blankets
- ☐ Snacks
- ☐ ....
- ☐ ....
- ☐ ....
- ☐ ....
- ☐ ....

Number these books to put them into size order, starting with the smallest. Make 1 the smallest and 5 the biggest.

CALM CORNER

FOOD FUN

Eating a balanced diet of healthy food, like fruit and veggies, can help give you more energy. Can you find the odd one out in each group?

PUT A CIRCLE AROUND THE ODD ONES OUT.

COLOR BY NUMBERS

Angry Ninja is feeling angry and doesn't want to share. Use the numbers in the key to color in this picture.

COLOR KEY

1
3
5

2
4
6

RAIN MAKER

The sound of rain can be super-relaxing to listen to. So, why not make your own rain shaker to calm you down when you're feeling angry?

ASK A GROWNUP TO HELP YOU.

YOU WILL NEED:

- ☐ A big plastic bottle or cardboard tube with a lid
- ☐ Uncooked rice
- ☐ Sticky tape to secure the lid

HOW TO MAKE IT:

1. Carefully pour the uncooked rice into the plastic bottle or tube until it's half full.

2. Pop the lid on tightly, and then tip it up and down slowly.

I sit quietly and use my rain maker to help me chill out.

KEEP COOL!

Do you ever get mad at the smallest thing and feel like you're about to explode? Check out these tips to help you find your calm when you're feeling frustrated and angry.

HERE ARE 10 TIPS FOR KEEPING YOUR COOL WHEN THINGS GET STRESSFUL. GIVE EACH TIP A SCORE FROM 1 TO 10 WHEN YOU TRY IT. 10 IS SUPER HELPFUL AND 1 IS NOT HELPFUL AT ALL.

Ground yourself by finding things you can see, smell, hear, feel, and taste.

SCORE EACH TIP HERE!

Find a space away from others and focus on your breathing. Keep it slow and steady, breathing in through your nose and out through your mouth.

Take a moment to step away from the situation and sit somewhere quiet.

Carry a sensory toy in your pocket, like a stress ball. Squeeze it whenever you feel tense.

Step away from the situation, close your eyes, and imagine that you are in your favorite place.

Repeat calm phrases in your head, like "cool down," or "give yourself a minute."

Write down what's making you mad on a piece of paper and tell yourself that you will look at it later.

Tell someone you trust about how you feel. Sharing your feelings can make you feel less alone.

FIVE STAR BREATHING

When something happens that makes you want to scream and shout, try Zen Ninja's special technique!

Trace your finger around the outline of the star and follow the instructions.

COLOR IN AND DECORATE THE STAR, TOO!

HOLD
BREATHE IN
BREATHE OUT
BREATHE IN
HOLD
BREATHE OUT
BREATHE IN
HOLD
BREATHE OUT
HOLD
BREATHE IN
BREATHE OUT
BREATHE IN
BREATHE OUT
HOLD

How did this activity make YOU feel?

Add a thumbs up or a thumbs down sticker here.

A TO Z OF ME!

If you're feeling frustrated or angry or just a little down, it helps to remind yourself of all the things that you are good at. Can you fill in each letter of the alphabet with a different activity or skill you do well?

A

B

C

D

E

F

G

H

I

J

K

L

M

N

O

P

Q

R

S

T

U

V

W

e X *ercise!*

Y

Z

ANGER DECODER

Help Angry Ninja crack this code from Calm Ninja. Use the key to reveal the hidden message.

Always remember this message when you feel like you might explode!

HOW TO DECODE THE MESSAGE:

● = E   ▬ = T   ▼ = I

■ = L   ⬡ = D   ☾ = H

▲ = C   ◣ = A   ✕ = N

★ = U   ◆ = O   ▱ = Y

⬠ = S

▱ ◆ ★   ▲ ◣ ✕

....

☾ ◣ ✕ ◆ ■ ●   ▬ ☾ ▼ ⬠

....

63

Can you help the ninjas clean up the classroom by finding all the items in the panel below?

ADD A NINJA STICKER NEXT TO EACH ITEM WHEN YOU SPOT IT IN THE BIG PICTURE.

ANGRY ME

Drawing when you feel angry can be a helpful way to let off steam and release negative energy. Draw what YOUR angry feeling looks like in the space below.

Perhaps your anger looks like a furious facial expression? Or maybe it looks like an explosion! It could even be a big, messy scribble using a color that you don't like!

Your angry feeling might look really messy and that's okay!

How did this activity make YOU feel?

Add a thumbs up or a thumbs down sticker here.

Now draw the opposite emotion in the area below. Perhaps it could be happy, calm, or excited. What does your opposite emotion look like?

DRAW A SMILEY FACE, A BEAUTIFUL RAINBOW, OR YOUR CALM PLACE.

You could fill this page with colorful swirls and pretty patterns, if that's how your mind feels when you're calm.

How did this activity make YOU feel?

Add a thumbs up or a thumbs down sticker here.

REFOCUS

Find a quiet spot away from others to try this breathing activity. Slowly follow the arrows with your finger as you breathe in and out.

BREATHE IN

BREATHE OUT

FILL IN THE PATH USING ANY COLORS THAT MAKE YOU FEEL CALM.

How did this activity make YOU feel?

Add a thumbs up or a thumbs down sticker here.

I use this when I feel nervous, and it helps to relax me.

NINJA SUDOKU

Get ready to focus your brain! Can you complete this grid using the remaining ninjas below? Write in the letters to show where each ninja fits in the grid. There should only be one of each ninja in every row, column, and small square.

RAGE RATING

Join Angry Ninja to put these mindfulness hacks to the test, and see which ones work best for you.

ANGER-METER

	ABOUT TO EXPLODE
	A LOT
	A LITTLE BIT
	NOT MUCH
	NOT AT ALL

Grab a colored pencil or crayon to record how angry you feel before and after trying one of these ideas. What will happen to your angry feelings?

BEFORE: HOW ANGRY ARE YOU RIGHT NOW?

NOW PICK ONE OF THESE TO TRY. WILL IT MAKE YOU FEEL LESS ANGRY? LET'S FIND OUT!

Do something to help someone else.

Write about a happy memory in your journal.

Breathe in and out slowly 10 times.

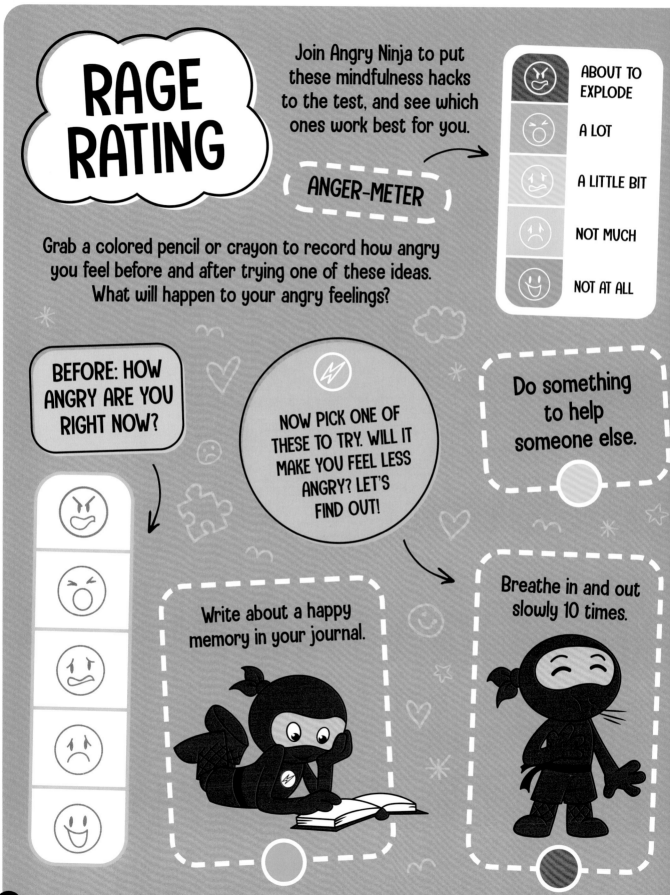

Find shapes in the clouds.

Write down 5 things you love about yourself.

Write down 5 positive things.

Practice your hobby.

HOW DID THIS EXERCISE MADE YOU FEEL? COLOR IN YOUR ANSWER OR DRAW YOUR EMOTION HERE.

Calm	Proud	Happy	Same as before

GIVE GRATITUDE

Find something to be grateful for every day to help your anger go away. Add a check mark next to each one as you go.

CHOOSE SOMETHING YOU'RE THANKFUL FOR EACH DAY AND TALK ABOUT IT WITH YOUR FAMILY!

- [ ] Your favorite family tradition
- [ ] A friend who always listens
- [ ] When you got better at something
- [ ] A movie you watched and loved
- [ ] Someone you can go to for advice
- [ ] A place that makes you feel calm
- [ ] A time when your friends surprised you
- [ ] When a teacher said "well done" to you
- [ ] Something that you are looking forward to
- [ ] An amazing book someone recommended
- [ ] When you overcame a fear
- [ ] A favorite memory
- [ ] You completed a task that you had been putting off
- [ ] A book that made you feel happy
- [ ] When somebody was kind to you
- [ ] When you used the energy from your anger to do something good
- [ ] A time you did something brave
- [ ] When you solved a problem with someone
- [ ] You used teamwork to complete a task
- [ ] Someone who always cheers you up

Use the space above to write about things you are grateful for, or draw pictures of them. Perhaps it's the people you live with, something someone gave to you, or a new skill you have learned!

HOW DO YOU FEEL?

If you are experiencing big feelings, don't give up. Use this feelings thermometer to help you figure out how you feel, then find a way to deal with it.

How do you feel?	What can you do about it?
ANGRY, FURIOUS, EXPLOSIVE Yelling, stomping, meltdown	Exercise, breathe deeply, count to 10
FRUSTRATED, ANNOYED, IRRITABLE Arguing, shutting down	Meditate, listen to music, exercise, ask for help
ANXIOUS, WORRIED, UNSETTLED Pacing, avoiding, clingy	Talk to someone, focus on what you can control, practice grounding by using your 5 senses
SAD, NEGATIVE, LONELY Crying, withdrawn, disengaged	Use positive self talk, chat to a friend, journal about your feelings
HAPPY, CALM, FOCUSED Smiling, laughing, engaged	Help someone else, do something fun. notice and enjoy your mood

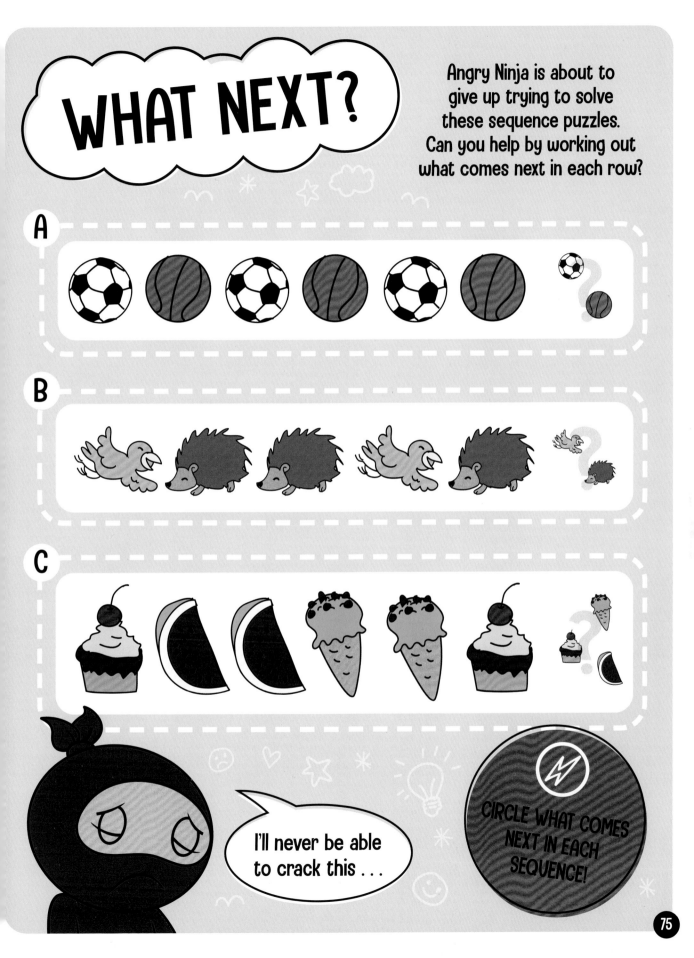

STRETCH IT OUT

Take time out and try these stretches. They'll give you more energy, and help you to cope when you feel overwhelmed. When you've tried them, rank the exercises from 1 to 4, with 1 being the most helpful.

Curl yourself up so you're round like a balloon.

RANKING

Stretch your arms and legs out wide like a star.

RANKING

SOMETIMES I FEEL ANGRY . . .

Finish the sentences using positive words about yourself. You can come up with your own ideas, or use the ones in the purple box below!

Sometimes I feel angry, but I ....

Sometimes I feel angry, but I ....

Sometimes I feel angry, but I ....

Sometimes I feel angry, but I ....

Check the ones that sound like you:

- ☐ . . . try my best
- ☐ . . . am kind
- ☐ . . . am funny
- ☐ . . . am generous
- ☐ . . . am good at sports

Answers:

PAGE 11: CLUES FROM WITHIN

PAGES 14-15: SEARCH AND FIND

PAGE 17: WORD SEARCH

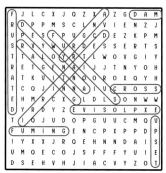

PAGES 18-19: CRACK THE CODES

"DRAW A PICTURE" "TAKE A TIME OUT"
"GO FOR A WALK"
"TAKE SOME DEEP BREATHS IN AND OUT"

PAGE 22-23: MAKE IT MATCH

PAGES 24-25: MAD MAZE

PAGE 26: SHADOW MATCHING

PAGES 30-31: CAN YOU SPOT IT?

PAGE 43 : HIDDEN MESSAGE
"ALWAYS REMEMBER TO BREATHE"

PAGE 47 : ODD ONE OUT-1. C, 2. B, 3. C

PAGES 54-55 : TO CALM CORNER

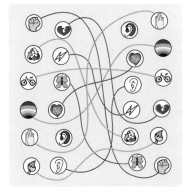

10 x NINJAS

PAGE 56: FOOD FUN

PAGE 57: COLOR BY NUMBER

PAGE 62: CHEER UP!

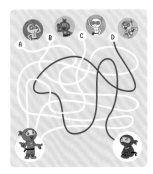

PAGE 63: ANGER DECODER
"YOU CAN HANDLE THIS"

PAGE 64-65: CLASS CLEANUP

PAGE 69: NINJA SUDOKU

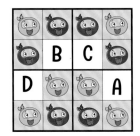

PAGE 75: WHAT NEXT?-A. SOCCER BALL,
B. HEDGEHOG, C. WATERMELON

PAGES 14–15: SEARCH AND FIND

HAPPY FACE STICKERS

PAGES 22–23: MAKE IT MATCH

PAGES 30–31: CAN YOU SPOT IT?

JUST FOR FUN STICKERS

EMOTION STICKERS: THROUGHOUT BOOK

JUST FO...

PAGES 64–65: CLASS CLEAN UP

EMOTION STICKERS: THROUGHOUT BOOK